CONSTRUCTION WORKERS

BY EMMA LESS

AMICUS READERS ● AMICUS INK

amicus
readers

Amicus Readers and Amicus Ink are imprints of Amicus
P.O. Box 1329, Mankato, MN 56002
www.amicuspublishing.us

Cataloging-in-Publication Data is on file with the Library of Congress.
ISBN 978-1-68151-291-4 (library binding)
ISBN 978-1-68152-273-9 (paperback)
ISBN 978-1-68151-353-9 (eBook)

Editor: Valerie Bodden
Designer: Patty Kelley

Photo Credits:
Cover: Kadmy/iStock
Interior: Adobe Stock: Lightfield Studios 3. Dreamstime.com: Stephen Coburn 4, Martinmark 6, Chode 8, Lightkeeper 10, James Steidl 13, Dmitry Shironosov 15, Michael Flippo 16TL, Hywit Dimyadi 16TR, Milosluz 16B.

Printed in China.

HC 10 9 8 7 6 5 4 3 2 1
PB 10 9 8 7 6 5 4 3 2 1

Bill's family is moving. Construction workers will make his house.

The worker looks
at plans.
They show how the
house will look.

This worker puts
on a hard hat.
It keeps
her head safe.

The worker uses
tools. She cuts
metal with a saw.
Look at the sparks!

This worker builds
the roof.
It takes lots of nails!

The worker adds pipes.
He adds wires, too.

The house is done.
It's time to move in!

SEEN AT A CONSTRUCTION SITE

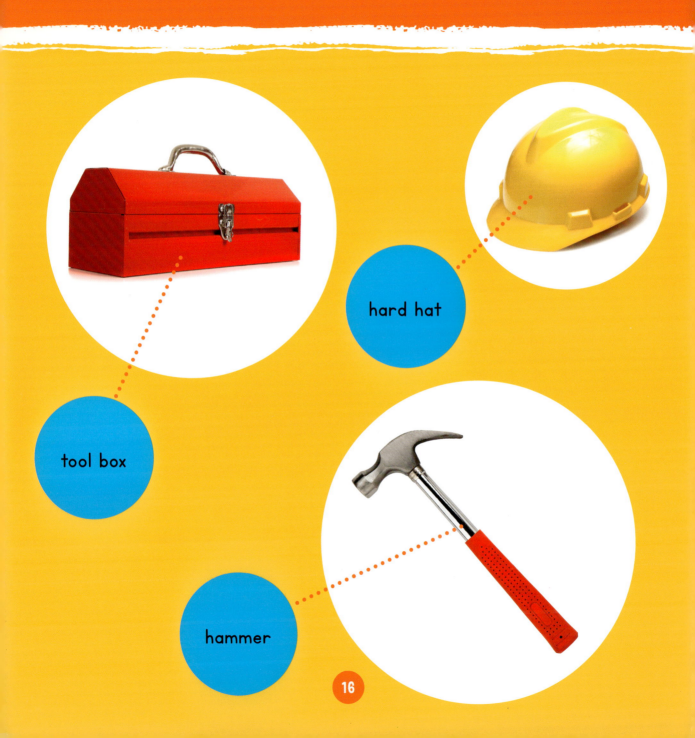

hard hat

tool box

hammer

16

2710